Who doesn't feel a little overwhelmed these days by the flood of advice, opinions, information overload and too many 'must-have' items?! It can often feel like we're being told what to do and think, in a way that can devalue our own views, our own feelings and our own ways of expression.

So here it is. Here are some blank pages, some uncluttered spaces. You may want to draw or write your own thoughts and feelings and aims – see what flows. Bring the light of insight into the world inside you, and around you.

This is your notebook. Enjoy the dance of pen or pencil on paper. And perhaps what now follows will be some very important pieces of the colourful puzzle that make up the unique picture of your life story…

We are given the title of human being on credit, but being human is a quest

Listen to the silence of the quiet space, inside of you

Enigma, wonder, awe and care light all the paths to truth

Each day the birdsong sounds its new tune, the sun rises afresh,
a new day awaits you. Nothing is yet written

We are on earth, but we live inside a whole universe
and contain its ingredients in us

You can light your own darkness

If we were in love with what we don't know, we would know so much more

True giving has no conditions, ever

We are so much better than what our experience in life
causes us to think and believe

We are what we accept and reject